As the
midnig
away, th
make is
reading

Lots of pigs = Hog-many!

By the same author

THE CHRISTMAS STOCKING JOKE BOOK
CYRIL'S CAT: CHARLIE'S NIGHT OUT
CYRIL'S CAT: & THE BIG SURPRISE
SANTA'S DIARY

In Young Puffin

THE FAIRY TALE JOKE BOOK
THE MIDNIGHT FEAST JOKE BOOK
READY TEDDY GO JOKE BOOK

THE LITTLE BOOK OF NEW YEAR'S RESOLUTIONS

PUFFIN BOOKS

PUFFIN BOOKS

Published by the Penguin Group
Penguin Books Ltd, 27 Wrights Lane, London W8 5TZ, England
Penguin Books USA Inc., 375 Hudson Street, New York, New York 10014, USA
Penguin Books Australia Ltd, Ringwood, Victoria, Australia
Penguin Books Canada Ltd, 10 Alcorn Avenue, Toronto, Ontario, Canada M4V 3B2
Penguin Books (NZ) Ltd, 182–190 Wairau Road, Auckland 10, New Zealand

Penguin Books Ltd, Registered Offices: Harmondsworth, Middlesex, England

First published 1993
10 9 8 7 6 5 4 3 2 1

Copyright © Shoo Rayner, 1993
All rights reserved

The moral right of the author/illustrator has been asserted

Printed in England by Clays Ltd, St Ives plc

Except in the United States of America, this book is sold subject
to the condition that it shall not, by way of trade or otherwise, be lent,
re-sold, hired out, or otherwise circulated without the publisher's
prior consent in any form of binding or cover other than that in which
it is published and without a similar condition including this condition
being imposed on the subsequent purchaser

NEW YEAR'S RESOLUTIONS SUGGESTIONS BOX

If your name is Bob then learn to swim.

If your name is Carol then keep practising until Christmas.

If your name is Mac then it's time to get a new raincoat.

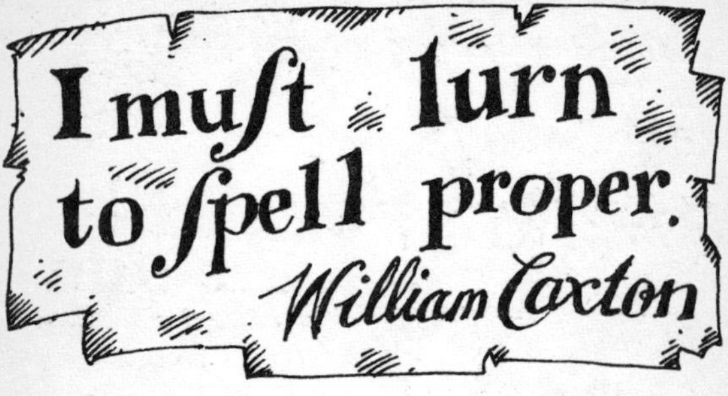

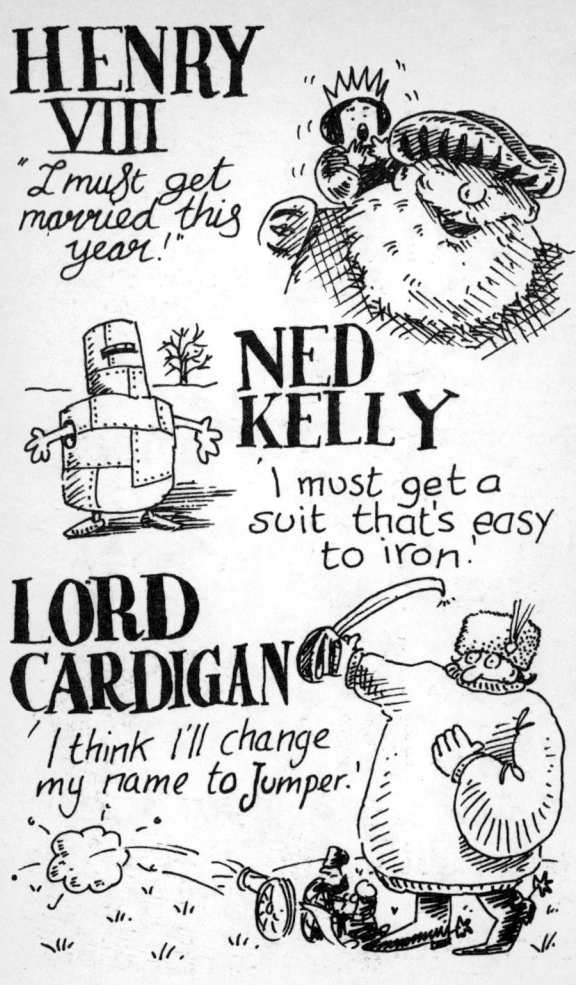

MUM'S NEW YEAR'S CHARTER

1. I will/will not have breakfast brought to me in bed every day.

2. I will/will not wave to my children as they set off on their five mile walk to school.

3. I will/will not go shopping for groceries every week.

4. I will/will not go shopping for new clothes every day.

5. I will/will not spend all day chained to the cooker trying to think of lovely and exciting new recipes to try out on my appreciative, gourmet family.

6. I will/will not get myself a job running a giant corporation, wear big shoulder pads and hire a child-minder!

7. I will/will not do the washing and cleaning and dusting and vacuuming and ironing. (DELETE AS APPLICABLE)

8. I will/will not keep fit by running ten miles a day and swimming 30 lengths, all before a breakfast of two dry biscuits and a glass of warm water.

9. I will/will not pamper myself with flowers and chocolates and bubble baths.

10. I will/will not probably carry on much the same as last year.

Signed _____

IF YOUR NAME IS...

RUSSELL
Then be quiet!

HEINZ
Then I've got 57 different resolutions for you!

BILL
Then try to get paid this year!

WANDA
Then stay where you are!

NEIL
Then stand up for yourself!

WILL
Then leave everything to me!

JUNE
Don't give up before half the year is out!

KURT
Don't be so short with people!

HOLLY
Don't be so prickly!

OSCAR
It's time you moved to Hollywood!

KIT
Then put yourself together!

HEADMASTER'S NEW YEAR'S REPORT

1. There will be free sweets every day.

2. No more punishments.

3. Choose which lessons you think will be best for you.

4. No more school uniform.

5. NO MORE GAMES.

6. Just do what you like.

PS These changes will take place as from 1 April.

SWIZZ!

Ancient wisdom for a modern world.

KONFUCIUS SAYS:

"This year will be like palm tree with 365 dates!"

"A bird's nest in the hand is worth two in the soup!"

"Barking dogs seldom bite unless they're barking mad!"

"Access hugs a car called Honda!"

"That'll do nicely sir!"

☆ FAMOUS ☆ RESOLUTIONS

'I'm going to give up smoking.' **Will Power**

'I'm going to get rich quick.' **Robin Banks**

'I'm going to stay out of trouble this year.' **Laura Norder**

'I will always tell the truth.' **Hebe Lying**

'I will never eat another sweet.'
Ashley I. Will

'I'm going on a diet.'
M.T. Tumtum

'We're going to holiday in Australia.'
Dick & Bill Platypus

'I'll never lend money again.'
U. Salome A. Pound

'I'm going to spend, spend, spend!'
Ivor Lottovitt

DAD'S
NEW YEAR'S CHARTER

- ❏ I promise that I will not be grumpy.

- ❏ I promise to put the shelves up, stop the tap dripping and do all those other little jobs around the place that need doing.

I promise to spend every day:
- ❏ in goal
- ❏ bowling for batting practice
- ❏ being a basketball hoop

- ❏ I promise to do all the cooking.

- ❏ I promise to put the rubbish out.

- ❏ I promise to do the cleaning and the washing up.

I promise to take everyone to:
- ❏ Alligator World
- ❏ Dinosaur Valley
- ❏ Cowboy Gulch
- ❏ Fairyland & Wonderworld
- ❏ On holiday

I promise to remember:
- ❏ Mum's birthday
- ❏ Gran's birthday
- ❏ Children's birthdays
- ❏ Wedding anniversary
- ❏ Other_____

Signed..

If your name is Gail
then try to calm down.

If your name is Seymour
then why don't you buy
a telescope?

If your name is Pat
then don't sit under cows!

If your name is Rob
then give it all back!

If your name is Dawn
then try to get up
early in the morning.

GREAT ARTISTIC RESOLUTIONS

Shakespeare

Here is a fragment of an old manuscript that was found down the back of the sofa in Anne Hathaway's cottage.

Picasso

Frankenstein
Will lend someone a hand.

E.T.
Promises to give his mother a phone call.

Mummies
Will try not to get so wrapped up in their work.

Burke & Hare
Will get some body to help them in their work.

Why wear yourself out when you

Know every day is much the same?

SLOBBOFAX
Jan 1

New Year's Day: got up ☐
had breakfast ☐ went out ☐
stayed in ☐ had lunch ☐
had tea ☐ stayed in and
watched television ☐
went out ☐ (where?..................)

weather ☼ ☐ ☁ ☐ ☔ ☐

Hot ☐ OK ☐ cold ☐ very cold ☐

Television was great ☐ ok ☐ bad ☐

meetings: ....
Notes: ....
Space for unusual occurrences.

A BROTHER'S NEW YEAR'S PROMISE LIST

○ I will always be kind.

○ I will always help with the washing and drying up.

○ I will always share my sweets / crisps / drinks, etc.

○ I will gladly lend my:
   ○ Toys
   ○ Games
   ○ Computer
   ○ Bike
   ○ Clothes
   ○ Homework
   ○ Support in times of trouble

Private KEEP OUT!

○ I will be served last and never ask for seconds.

○ I will go to bed at night and read quietly until it's time to turn out the lights.

○ I will always help Mum when she asks. *(I'll even tidy up my room once in a while!)*

○ I will always help Dad when he asks. *(That includes holding bits of wood that he's sawing, washing the car, passing tools and demolishing walls when they need it!)*

○ I will not squeeze my spots!

○ I will bash anyone who reads this!!!!!

Signed..

BRILLO RESSIES!

> "I'm going to have BRILLIANT ideas."
> Les R. Beams

> "I'm going to earn more money than I know what to do with."
> Billy Onns

> "I'm going to do some serious scientific experiments this year."
> Rhys Urch

> "We're going to cross America."
> Harry Zona, Mary Land, Ida Hoe
> Al Asker and Ken Tuckey

> "I'm going to stand out from the crowd."
> Anne X. Entrick

> "I'm going to rule the world!"
> Maggie Lomania

> "I'm going to stop asking stupid questions."
> Juno Watt

A SISTER'S NEW YEAR'S PROMISES

1. I promise not to leave fluffy things down the back of the sofa.

2. I promise I will let my brother join in when I play football, cricket, baseball, marbles and cops and robbers.
   (Delete as applicable)

3. I promise not to giggle.

4. I promise not to laugh at my brother's spots.

5. I promise that I won't wear anything pink for at least a year.

6 I promise to help with:
The washing up.
The cleaning.
The gardening.
The lawn-mowing.
The car washing.
(Delete as applicable)

7 I promise not to hide the TV remote control when my favourite programme is on.

8 I promise not to gossip and share secrets with my friends. *(Well, not much!)*

Signed..

YOUR YEAR IN THE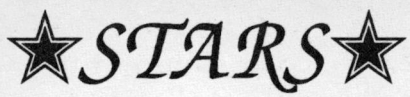

Capricorn ⛥   *22 Dec-20 Jan*
Being an old goat can be hard to come to terms with. The best thing you can do this year is find a Nanny to look after you, then you can Billy well do what you like. Lucky number: 242.

Aquarius ≈   *21 Jan-19 Feb*
With a watery sign like yours, you are probably going to the seaside for your holidays. This may not be such a good idea as you may well find yourself getting wet. It will rain a lot for you this year. Lucky colour: blue. Lucky number: 3.

Pisces ♓ 20 Feb-20 Mar

You've got your fish finger in too many ocean pies. If you don't cast about this year you'll have haddock for good. You will fall in love; hook, line and sinker.
Lucky colour: sea green.

Aries ♈ 21 Mar-20 Apr

Being a ram, your skull is very thick. You can bash it against brick walls as much as you like, you won't feel a thing, but then, neither will the wall!
Lucky herb: mint.

Taurus ♉ 21 April-21 May

You go at life like a bull in a china shop. Need I say more?
Lucky food: Yorkshire Pudding.
Lucky colour: red.

Gemini   22 May-21 June
This is going to be a good time for both of you. If you're in two minds about a decision just remember: two heads are better than one. Lucky number: 2.

Cancer   22 June-23 July
The sign of the lobster in the new moon is telling you to stop going sideways. Lucky mineral: sand.

Leo   24 July-23 Aug
Take pride in yourself and put your head in the sharp-toothed jaws of an uncertain future. Lucky beast: unicorn.

Virgo   24 Aug-23 Sept
This year you will do lots of

things for the first time.
Lucky colour: white.

Libra 24 Sept-23 Oct

You may be feeling unbalanced at the moment. This is well within the normal scale of things, even though you may be weighed down on one side.
Lucky animal: very scaly fish.

Scorpio 24 Oct-22 Nov

The sting's the thing!
Lucky sign: heads or tails.

Sagittarius 23 Nov-21 Dec

You are right on target for gold this year. Wear a dickie bow and you should have the world all of a quiver! Lucky beast: centaur.

IF A JOB'S WORTH DOING...

Cobblers will cease being down at heel.

Politicians will tell the truth.

Photographers will focus on developing their careers.

Gardeners will turn over a new leaf.

Drivers will follow the straight and narrow.

Train drivers will try not to go off the rails.

Astronauts will boldly go where no man has gone before.

Sewage men will boldly go!

Runners will put their best feet forward.

Fishermen will catch the ones that got away!

MORE GREAT ARTISTIC RESOLUTIONS

Michelangelo
Painting the Sistine Chapel Ceiling

"I think I'll have a little lie down."

Greta Garbo

this year I vish to be alone

Henry Ford

I'm going to make so many cars there won't be any room left to drive them!

A PET'S NEW YEAR'S CONTRACT

****

1. I promise to be soft, fluffy and huggable.

2. I promise to be friendly and not to dribble over people.

3. I promise to be cute and stupid.

4. I promise to guard the house from burglars, window cleaners, friends and relations.

5. I promise not to scratch the furniture.

6. I promise not to go whoopsie on the carpet.

7. I promise to be a loving faithful friend.

Place paw or claw print here. →

Luke...Get some glasses.

Sandy...Always be shore!

Tel...Phone your mum.

Ernie should make an honest living!

WET PAINT

Art.

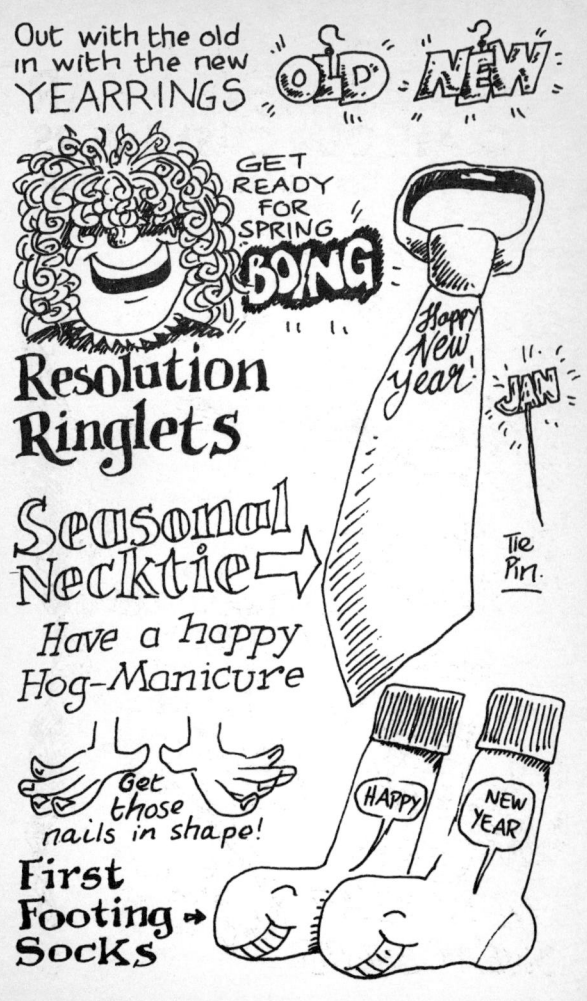

> I'm going to learn how to sing.
> Carrie O'Key

> I'm going to buy a motorbike.
> Rev. Yamota

> I'm going to carpet the whole house.
> Walter Wall

> I'm going to get a knighthood.
> Neil Down

> I'm going to find out what's the matter with me.
> Di Agnosis

MY NEW YEAR'S RESOLUTIONS

I WILL: YES   NO

Work hard......................☐   ☐

Stop eating sweets............☐   ☐

Have a bath once..............☐   ☐
in a while

Help in the kitchen...........☐   ☐

Help around the house...☐   ☐

Help in the garden...........☐   ☐

Be nice to grannies/.......☐   ☐
grandads/aunties/uncles
(Delete as applicable)

Be nice to brothers	☐	☐
Be nice to sisters	☐	☐
Save/spend all my pocket money	☐	☐
Say thank you	☐	☐
Say please	☐	☐
Say I beg your pardon	☐	☐
Behave myself in public	☐	☐
Wait my turn	☐	☐
Remember to clean my teeth	☐	☐
Be kind to animals (This does not include little brothers or sisters!)	☐	☐

Use this space to write your own special New Year's Resolution...............

Signed..

Good luck
and
a very happy New Year